# Lucky
# Bones

**PITT POETRY SERIES**

Ed Ochester, Editor

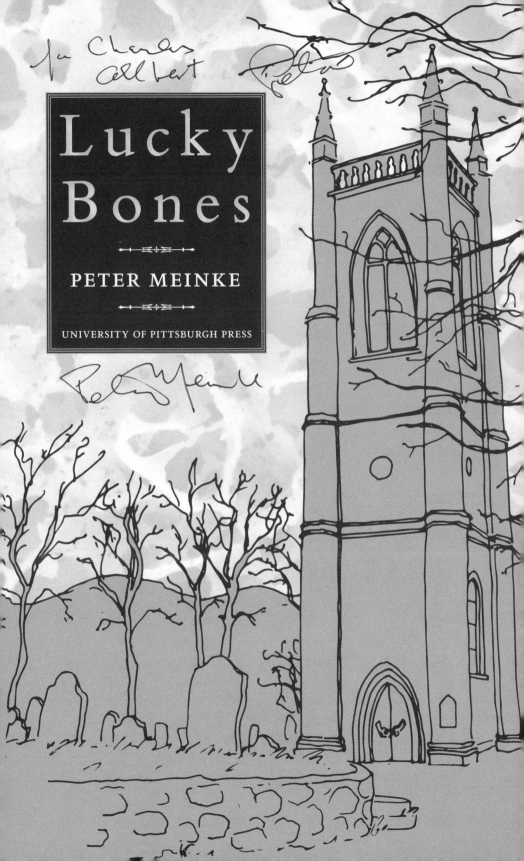

# Lucky
# Bones

## PETER MEINKE

### UNIVERSITY OF PITTSBURGH PRESS

Published by the University of Pittsburgh Press, Pittsburgh, Pa., 15260

Manufactured in the United States of America

Printed on acid-free paper

10 9 8 7 6 5 4 3 2 1

ISBN 13: 978-0-8229-6310-3

ISBN 10: 0-8229-6310-8

for Paul Zimmer, Ed Ochester, and Richard Mathews:

long-time friends and editors *extraordinaires*

# Contents

## II. SKIPPING STONES

## OLD HOUSES

Old houses
are best they have secrets
shadows trembling everywhere
in closet and corner   their weaknesses secret
cracks in the blocks   corroded pipes   the termites' patient
gnawing   Their strengths are secret too:   the handcarved
attic beam   the portrait paneled over   a feeling they've
earned their way   Every board in the house has been
pressed   by finger and foot   forehead and knee   tears on
old tiles have worn their stories   stories spread through
the rooms   like the hint of camellias   we   breathe stories
here we inhale old passions   exhale the dead resolutions
that are still   moving   In the closet there is . . .   something
Sun slants through casement windows   around slender
candles   shattering   on the wicker where we sit   in love
with the shadows   old houses are best old oaks bend over
them   whispering it's all right it's all right   all those kids
had fun   and remember that young couple   who had such
love for each other it overflowed and   did the azaleas sing
and birds blaze like roses ?   and even the garage
long ago burned down   was   an object of affection

# I. THE MOLECULE OF LIFE

## DRIVE-BY SHOOTINGS

What kind of world do we live in?  you asked
when our neighbor's house  newly painted
burned to the ground  reasonless arson

What kind of world do we live in?

A city I know has a wooden fence with a hole in it  People pedal by on bikes  drop
some money in the hole  stick in their arms  get a shot  and wobble away
sometimes  getting hit by cars  the same needle  all afternoon

That's the kind of world we live in

# THE FIREBUG

The building's old  anyway  and deserves to burn
the walls dark with blood and age  the dry taps laced with rust

the face brown and ugly  The architect's dead  his plans splay open

the pages curl together   And fire's so beautiful  blue and red:
*the building deserves this beauty*   the firebug said

# CASSANDRA IN THE LIBRARY

*Blood is simple   books complex:*
*the drone of professors drowned by the roar of sex*

Plato's dust before Virginia's thighs
Shakespeare pales beside her breathing breast
Voltaire's wit wilts beneath her eyes
Poetry nor wisdom withstands the test
of blood:  when mind and body clash
the mind's the one whose opposition's rash

*Killing's liquid   work's dust*
*our craving for passion quenched by a crimson lust*

What can an office offer but a cursed
routine  an inane trivial bore?
A water cooler doesn't slake the thirst
of blood that rages for a taste of war:
a horde of disappointed men have dreams
fired by bursting flares and female screams

*Action releases   thought confines*
*we'll burst into blood again   O see the signs*

The cauldron seethes   boiling black white
yellow red and brown in a poisoned brew
swallowed by nations spoiling for a fight
The last great sword tilts like a rotten tooth
so write down this  write it in blood
to guide the creatures crawling from the mud:

*You who inherit the earth  after we drown*
*learn to walk on water  or turn around*

In Florida  mottled birdwatchers screech brakes
to see an ivory-billed woodpecker bang away
on a dying bay  *Not many left  Peter  not many*
*left*  Forests shrink  flocks disappear  Birdwatchers
worry where we're heading
*but over all our hills the birdlike generals are*
*spreading . . .*

In Sunset Lake a thick pike trailing hooks and
leaders bends stubbornly in diminishing circles
jaw locked in its Nemonian smile  Water tastes
different now: so do fish  Fishermen claim
their schools are thinning
*but under all our seas the fishlike generals are*
*grinning . . .*

In battening churches  God's crowded out
The pulpits reflect the pews reflect the
pulpits reflect the . . .  Who's the Warden
to teach us how to choose?  Coarse Christians
muscle in: Hey Big Fella  move your Ass
*and throughout the firmament the godlike generals*
*make things come to pass*

## HABEMUS PAPAM

O goodum!   *Habemus Papam*
who'll soon intone
the usual crapam

and the poor poor will weepum

and the rich will yawn
and eatem
like pablum

# ARS LONGA, VITA BREVIS

Now that I've reached the age
when I stumble up the stage
for my job-concluding pin
every evening out's a chore
Looking forward to my gin
I think  with resigned regret
as I trip the final step
my *vita*'s not so *brevis* any more

*Mortúus* my youthful storms
all melancholy gone
those clouds are sucked away
on soundtracks of Marianne
and Eleanor Rigby dreams
I remember a ribbon on the floor
but what were my girl friends' names?
My sweetheart isn't *Mavis* anymore

America rolls like a pig
in dirty oil and gore
*My country my pig* I shout
to the stars whose blinking snouts
and planetary snuffles
uproot the universe
as they gather galactic truffles . . .
My *mentis* isn't *compos* any more

Looking around the world
why do I feel so gay
when I'm not gay at all

A martini's not strong enough
to block the world's fat fist
so what's the olive for
and the lemon's bitter twist?
My *gravitas* curls groveling on the floor

I dream of my old aunts still
bending over their cards
Nana and Lizzie and Lil
They pressed me against their hearts
I could hardly get my breath
Then they shooed me out the door
to my certain death:
My *vita*'s not so *brevis* any more

# HABEUS CORPUS

We used to sing Pete Seeger's
"Guantánamera"
meaning 'woman from Guantánamo'

but now the men there
have stopped eating
and sing 'Where's my *corpus*?'

while doctors push pain
by enteral feeding
which doesn't stop the bleeding

from their non
existent
veins

# SIC TRANSIT GLORIA MUNDI

Looking hard and singing loud  we rode the BMT
from Flatbush Avenue to Ebbets Field
going to Dodgers games   My forehead peeled

from bathing in the bleacher's sun   free
for members of the Police Athletic League
teenaged hoodlums hoping the day might yield

a fight  a feel  a pocketbook of coins  *Sic
transit* is what I think   Once bright and quick
the teams and days have left for lesser places

since we were young and violent  the boys
of summer rounding the puffed-up bases
making a joyful noise

## FIVE LANDAYS WITH A LATIN PHRASE

### I. E Pluribus Unum
*E pluribus unum*: old penny
doled by the greathearted few to the grateful many

### II. The Chicken Hawk Addresses His Constituents
'This war will last *ad infinitum*'
he brayed: 'We need your help.'   'Take *these*' we said 'and
bite'm'

### III. Guiding Wisdom
He tried to live by his minimum
*magnum opus*: 'Don't be a goofus  or a dopam'

### IV. Two Gentlemen of Verona
He said 'Thou canst quote me  Verbatim'
'I shall not' quoth V 'but thou canst quote *me* verbatim'

### V. Café Scene
'Can't resist this éclaire—is that so
bad?' the plump man pleads   She glares: '*Ipso facto*, Fatso'

## HEARTWORLD

. . . each night alone   my heartbeat magnified in a vast hall   and I can feel
all the hearts in the world thumping on every side:   the hearts of mice and
moles   ferrets and fish   I'm smothered in hearts   7 billion just counting
humans   the others countless   a massive universal mound
a throbbing orchestra of clams and snails and heaped anemones fighting
off the dark with the drum and fife at the bottom of all music:
my*life* my*life* my*life* my*life* . . .

## PATTY'S FATHER

"Sweet guy," she said, "wrote one letter his whole life":
*Dear Patty, Last night I finished the fudge*
*then watched TV; Robert & his new wife*
*dropped by for a drink (we didn't drink that much!).*
*Letters are hard to write! All my love, Dad*

One week later  on a perfectly safe plane
an inner membrane popped  spraying blood:
arterial bombardment of the brain
that left him not her father  just a breather
plugged in the uncharged void:  nobody home
She cried to God:  not home there either
heaven and hell in a semiprivate room

Still  we're blessed  though no one sees or hears
by all impermanent grief & her mammalian tears

## D. E. A. T. H.

At the wrong time  Death rang to take
him away  *Not ready* he said  grabbing
the door  *my stocks are up and anyway*
*I'm bigger* This was true: Death was maybe
5'2" on tiptoe  with a little pot

*Cuts no ice I gotta bring you in*
The shrimp had rusty handcuffs  rattled them
at Charlie like a sleazewad bounty hunter
Where were Charlie's wife  his kids  the rotten
neighbors?  Nobody pulled his weight these days

He should have charged the bastard
grabbed his skinny neck  and thrown
the cuffs away  but felt light-headed
somehow  faintly nauseous: his breath
came shallow  fast  his hands and forehead cold

*Who says you gotta  I mean* have to
*bring me in?* said Charlie  falling back
on dignity  voice stubborn but unsteady—
*Tell him I am not ready!*—dropping
contractions in his corporate manner

*I love it when they whine* Death muttered
snapping on the cuffs and yanking Charlie
wheezing toward the door  By the time they got out
the lawn  the street  the Oldsmobile were gone
*Who?* Charlie gargled  damp as cheese  *Who?*

Death's voice grated like a lacy muffler  *Ah Boss*
*is woiser than me* he said  *and littler  I'm just*
*his Anagram  his muscle-mime: remember*
*how you liked to curl your lip?  He's the one*
*in you who  H. A. T. E. D.  Get it?*

That was too neat  like Charlie's room in Hell
where nothing could be moved  at least not
far  It took two hands to lift a pencil: before he
could write the "H" in H. E. L. P.  it snapped back down
He saw that this would take a lot of time

# THE FAMILY MEGASHELTER SONG, 1961

### As sung to a rockabilly tune

*55 years ago, Governor Nelson Rockefeller sponsored a compulsory nuclear
bomb shelter plan for all American homes; we may have come full circle*


. . . I think we're ready   We have a lovely shelter
and can hardly wait to hear the bomb explode
It's planned with care   we've not been helter-skelter:
please notice our collapsible commode

It'll be a little crowded  with us five:
my wife  two lively kids  Grandma and me
but we've a plan to keep us all alive
and I pass it on to fellow targets  free

The secret is: use pills   They're very small
and can be kept in paper  wood  or tin
We have pills to quiet babies when they bawl
and pills to poison neighbors who pop in

Pills to keep the kids asleep for days
pills to cure the dog of worms and rabies
pills to calm poor Grandma's nervous phase
and pills to keep my wife from having babies

So  in our little pillbox underground
we'll be equipped as well as any king
and while the world comes crashing all around
the five of us will sit and laugh and sing . . .

My only worry is that  in the dark
things might get turned around  and then just maybe
the dog will fall asleep  the kids will bark
my wife get worms  and Grandma have the baby . . .

# GRASSHOPPERS OF THE WORLD, UNITE

From fields of rice & poppies
from fortresses of stone
maniac asylums
where skin flakes off the bone
from Kabul and Jerusalem
rings a fiercely joyous sound:
*merrily we mow them down*
*mow them down*
*mow them down*
*merrily . . .*

dead men in shallow beds pop up to say
Life is essentially frivolous & gay

*Gaiety's an element*
*blazing in the tenement*
*bouncing off the hot cement*
*and under skirts with lewd intent*

Christ enjoys our laughter but God wants us to pay
Life is essentially frivolous & gay

Churchy fathers in their chairs
bend their necks and say their prayers
Children frown with hands on knees
watching plastic birds & bees
Ladies sitting stiff & straight
lock the latch of heaven's gates
the world infernally assays
to light a dark and serious blaze

but Buddha knows it's just as well
to fan the flames of whatthehell

Paupers in the flophouses tippling away:
Life is essentially frivolous & gay

Look at the ant  they say  he does
his work  ready for December's day
Now the grasshopper  he may play
but winter comes & then he'll cough
and freeze his little thorax off
cuts down on the music   Still I say
I say the grasshopper's right in a fundamental way:
Rub your legs together folks now's the time to play

*Though virgins sulk and ministers shout*
*and artists mutter when they're sober*
*earth rejects the serious Fausts*
*and loves the gay & zesty Zorbas*

On sandy beaches young girls sun like seals
Everywhere fathers are pitching to their sons
Frisbees spin through haze like psychedelic halos:
While nations divide and war multiplies
lovers gaze in lovers' eyes
laughter ripples through the fields and HEY
life is essentially frivolous & gay
Sing this till the point is made
Life is  etc. . . . (repeat ad lib & fade)

# ELECTION DAY 2012

After the rain the lizards preen
on the heavy leaves  the bent grass
Our Lizard of the Mail Box pokes out his slim head
craning this way and that   *Where's the mail?*
*Is it National Lizard Day or what?*
The chameleon crawls from inside
the mouth of our terra cotta wood sprite
and hangs like a rusty tongue to lick

the rough pine boards of our deck
And from the screened-in pantry sink
the thin feet of our tiny Cuban grip
the grill my wife leans there
to help him see what he's missed:
it's cooler now  the wind's picking up   Nearby
the gutters run deceptively clean

and the green anole on our daily *Times*
dips its long snout in droplets scattered
over the blue plastic bag
hiding the headlines from us all
Can he see motion in the alley
where the broken glass glitters

and the drunks are pissing blood?
Every Large One armed against everyone
unlike himself  females circling
the muscled males with their sharp teeth?
O my quiet lizards  brown and black

skink and gecko  gaudy iguana
O all of you green and mottled
be careful:  watch your tails
while somewhere  deep and disguised

in a dark Columbian rainforest
guarding its expanding nation
the Jesus Christ Lizard

runs across water  its eyes
seeing everything at once

and not with adoration

# ANTS, ANTS

. . . the holes surprise us
showing up as we lop section after

section  something has mined
the heart of this live oak

its hard body
riddled with tunnels  a cancer

scribbling its nibbling question
only the saw can answer  And now

spitting grain like foam
the steel teeth knock on wood

and enter: no one home  . . .

. . . but in the last section  there
they are  black bodies racing

down dark lanes just
ahead of the saw's whine and bite

an ant stampede  piling in the end
like cattle at a canyon wall  When

we pick it up they boil out
*our hands! our arms!*

and we fling that log
that live wire

first on the ignorant fire  . . .

## THE STORM

Our dogwood  whose buds open up
like chalices of baby peas  crashed down
and even we don't care: we're searching
for two who drowned in Thursday's storm
Limbs splintered  the tree sprawls

across our lawn  raking our tulip
bed  We *think* the men have drowned:
the slim ketch they called *Sea King*
with fishermen's bravado  bobbed home
keel up  to harbor among the yawls

and sloops and all the lucky ships
outriding killer winds  The town
feels sick: an arbitrary thing
this dragging down  Hard to blame
the lake  the graceful boat . . . Though no one's fault

it stings us like a slap
across the face from someone
we trusted  Subdued in church  we sing
"Morning Has Broken" ashamed
that we can sing at all

that in a world so easy to slip
from  we remain  not only not undone
but healthy  strong and prospering
by ducking water  wind and flame:
though faintly  from afar  atonement calls

Back home  the dogwood's branches grip
the grass like a soldier taken
in mid-charge  little rings
of dirt around each point   Someone's aim
was good:  Time for the ax and saw

## A FABLE: THE FLOSS-SILK TREE AND THE PHILODENDRON

In Brazil they call the floss-silk *palo borracho*
'drunken tree' because each blossom opens
like a provocative dancer at Carnaval

and though the philodendron's
a low and homely vine  it still winds upwards
along the thorny trunk toward the swaying flowers
a blue-collar Orpheus straining for his Eurydice
its small leaves swelling alarmingly
like the hearts of wanton gods

For what's love but recognizing beauty
as a temporary gift and strangling it
against all odds?

## MIRROR LAKE

Delicate & clean
as Japanese brush & ink
the plump inland gulls

wear deceptively
neutral tones   Splashes of black
at beak  tail  & eye

pin to the landscape
their formal gray wings & back:
soft white crown  neck  breast

pose for the artist
on jointed pencil-pipe legs
models of mildness:

but the eyes are mean
the black beaks nasty-hooked   Tough
little buggers  they

strut  make ducks duck  and
buzz the endangered behinds
of plump pelicans

## THE LOVER

When I was young
blood-driven and obsessed
by devils bucking in my veins
I burned to be caressed

*Old bones & flesh*
*I'll beat you yet*

Scarlet skirts that blazed
like capes before a bull
would make me paw the earth:
I felt so powerful

Now my blood is dust
but still my slower pulse
throbs to the beat of lust
with less results

*Old bones & flesh*
*I'll beat you yet*

I may not ever get
the philosophic mind
though winter's ice will set
and ice is blind

When I'm old
bed-ridden & forgiven
by women wrapped in shawls
I'll repent & go to heaven

and when I see God dancing
I'll tell Her like a friend
God  the game's worth the candle
but tiring  in the end

*Old bones & flesh*
*I'll beat you yet*

# BABYLON

Years ago

we camped in a northern field:
The snow   Her snow-white skin   By the black
oaks we leaned together and looked back:
Our steps alone leading from tree to tree
shadowed that surface with a darker white

All afternoon icicles glittered
like frozen gardens in Babylon

And still today
when I see snow broken by boots
in a white sun  my heart shivers
with wonder and her voice cries in the cold
the words slanting like sleet on fire:

*We will be together forever  from this day on!*

# LUCKY BONES

He's a sight  the old athlete
bent at 78

hopping crow-like to peck
a ball on the short bounce

dropping it dead over the net
in open court   *Great shot!*

his partner shouts  but
he can't hear   Instead

his birdneck swivels
toward his wife

who used to toss car keys
that flashed through light

like lucky bones crying  *Hey
big fella  think fast!*

and he thinks *That's
just the past in my head*

*like a red-eyed crow*
and he's thinking *Christ*  he

could still catch them if she
were still there to throw

## FLOATERS

When the shadow of a bird began winging
across my right eye  I tried to zero in
just to see what was bothering me: it soared
like a small hawk maybe  wringing the high cold
air with its curved claws  but when it froze at last
in my sight  flattened motionless before me

I could see it was just an insect on my
lens  with spidery legs splayed out as if it
had landed hard  and now there was another
and another I yanked off my glasses in
disgust  but there they were  still crawling across

my eye like fleas zigzagging through Death Valley
and it took a month until I was told by
a fuzzily cheerful ophthalmologist
that they were only small patches of protein

torn from my aging retina  floating like
black syllables through the vitreous humor
which I also failed to see  He said it's just

something expected as flaky old age tugs
us toward debris  Therefore  in retrospect I

can tell you I would have preferred hawks or bugs

## THE ACTIVIST

for Jeanne


No one so impractical:  you're
my endangered specie  Carolina
parakeet  pileated woodpecker
You'd give those perfect teeth to find a
passenger pigeon or spotted owl
cooing and hooting at the carved feet
of our bed   And Save the whales!   you shout
while legal harpoons launch off lowering fleets

The world's autotoxic:  from a sick center
deserts spread like cancer across its dented surface
making you right about everything  my mimosa
my warbler   Still I confess  when you enter
our room with blazing eyes  biodiversity's
a distant star:  global warming's closer

## FRONT-RHYMED EASTER ANTI-SONNET

Sonnets have had it: dead as yellow
birds bobbing like buoys on pink Easter
bonnets   Bad enough you have to use
words without sinking the buggers in fourteen
lines   O Shakespeare Milton   what made you
choose them?   O Formalist  can't you read the
signs?   O Meinke  why are you writing another?
Who's sick of sonnets?   Iamb   iamb

And true  I also have had it:  taught too
much Bishop  Wilbur  Frost   It all shows   Through
blue-black spring evenings I shouldn't think of
such old tugs as sonnets when damn it the stars
tack blazing through the sky   Miraculous! Mir-
aculous!  on their traditional track to glorify

## POEM ON YOUR BIRTHDAY

We always love the poem we're working on
we like the sounds of it
consonants and vowels
floating off our ballpoint pens
as if they were going somewhere important

Right now  I'm so excited
by this very poem
I have to summon your soft touch
to calm me down
After all   we remind ourselves
tomorrow  I may not like it so much

But it's no use: I love it today
with my primitive heart
wingless as an *Apteryx*
Hey poem  come down to me
Make this day a special day:
the twenty-fifth of March
two thousand and six

## FATHER AND CHILD

Our snow-white daughter juggles poisoned apples
sweeps ashes happily with Cinderella
how deep she sleeps the sleep of Sleeping Beauty
while froggy princes hop around her tower

She has no trouble telling good from evil:
the warts and scratchy voices give away
those mean in spirit   goblins and the devils
who laugh and cackle first  but later pay

Identifying always with the beauties
she smiles to see the witches melt like snow
while kings grow gaunt among their scarlet rubies:
How can we leak the secret that we know?

*Child  love the cruel and ugly older sisters*
*who crawl into the forest to die alone*
*for look  my mouth is filled with toads and vipers*
*your hands  wrinkled like a crone's*

## THE DEVIL'S PAINTBRUSH

*Hieracium aurantiacum*: "a bad weed
in pastures and waste places"

Before we met  I used to write at night
puffing like a fiend  my row of pipes by
a whisky glass in a dim pool of light:
a smoky reeky bubble in the room
where nothing could be seen below my waist
or above the desklamp's copper snakelike stem
a self-contained and brain-eroding system

Outside the bubble  voices in the night
pressed sibilant  insistent  but a waste
of time and effort if they thought that by
just calling they'd pull me from that room
behind my eyes  focused on this inner light
or rather *darkness* . . .

It wasn't light
I realize now  Like a pilot as he stems
the encroaching tide  perched in a little room
above the deck  I wrote of *weeds blood night
death loneliness that money couldn't buy*:
our long catechism of human waste . . .

In short I was a bore  We *all* can smell the waste
we drown in—infants lost for lack of light
lands for lack of courage  disease that coughs nearby
the bleeding that no bandages can stem—
but those were my subjects as I scrawled all night
inside the bubble in our living room

And now   you open all the other rooms
around me  these Edens  and the different ways
our guiltless children breathe   The gobs of night
break up like ice in April   light
blessing all  from snake to applestem
until my devils fled and spit good-bye

But  how to write without them?   *There's the rub*   I
couldn't work inside a bright-lit room
and so began in dusky morning   pipestem
and whisky glass untouched  An awful waste
I thought  learning slowly to love the light
and slowly blinking  rubbing off the night

Now  I can sleep at night  though from this room
by spotted daylight daisies  still can see
the devil's paintbrush on its wasting stem

# THE MOLECULE OF LIFE

The table I drown at  the rug the table's on
the window curtains  all are matching blue
reflecting the cool wavelength of light our eye
discerns welling between violent and green

On the wall hangs a print  *The River Oise*
*Near Pontoise*  whose marine sky and stream
mirror each other like an echo of the room
filling this space with blue as water fills a pool

Pissarro wanted to be scientific:
his blues vibrate behind moving clouds
or below the rippled images of tree
and smokestack  white wall  red roof

On canvas he strove for the sparkle  swirl
the molecule of life and always  somewhere
through gray haze or the bent sunlight
of a meadow  placed a figure  solid

but full of grace  composed  like the leaves
and rocks and living wood  with short strokes
of pure color—no black or white at all—as in God's
first blueprint of the world before the flood

## II. SKIPPING STONES

# EMILY DICKINSON THINKS ABOUT BUYING A RIBBON

I'm all elbow – and angle
But my neck's fine   It can
Justify – a ribbon

I would like to get Red –
Vermillion
But Father would disapprove

A serious Blue – then – worn loose
Like a Lover's knot
A decent one could strangle

With it – I'd have wine
Not the barrell'd rum of Father's
Then – let Him come –

## BELGIAN TRUFFLES

A Tart's Love Song

I bought Belgian chocolates for my beau
dark truffles to entice his tongue
and all his senses top to toe
My hungry eyes with longing clung
at closest range to each sweet part:
the flaring nostril  flushing cheek
all rushing from his racing heart
until my beau could barely speak

His chin  his throat:  the chocolate's job
was almost done  the climax near—
and when his Adam's apple bobbed
in ecstasy  I gasped *Mes chères!*
to those who made my heart-throb throb:

*Neck-lust and the chocolatière*

# JULIET 2010

I'd have preferred it the other way:
Juliet did it so cleanly  so well

What half-hearted measures never could say
the rude unchangeable act would tell
Love's no longer that absolute thing
wild with folly and laughter and fear

Romeo's voice has a practical ring:
he rubs my shoulders and dries my tears

Last sacraments once were the parting gift
Let's spare each other that Veronese test
We'll compromise and part and drift
to other loves and safer beds

Then you in your village and I in mine
can swallow these crumbs with the local wine

## UNBEARABLE LIGHTNESS

Her step was so light we imagined
wings of hummingbirds lifting her shoulders
as her toes brushed the ground
leaving faint scuff marks as she flew
O  to her boyfriend crying *Love*
*is endless and forever young!*

in hummingbird tongue

But he weighed her down
with rings and excuses brassy as blue jays
so she stamped and stamped
while he flew circles around her
until he tired and coasted home
and they each pecked a pledge

like lovebirds in a cage

and showered each other with bracelets
necklaces lockets as they feathered their nest
till they could hardly move
Then each step struck the earth like stone
and their finally feet took root
breaking the surface at last

while the moles labored past

## CHRISTMAS BURNING

The souvlaki joint on the Boardwalk
just burned down: an offering
of smoke and ice   Now no one's near
The Coppertone girl blesses from the pier
A lone sparrow scratches everywhere:
the pipes are frozen

*She told him she'd be here*

The old hotels are cold and drafty
They must have been tacky
even in the twenties
all those curves and glitter
Now they pray for Mafia money
to make them better

*She told him someone told her*
*she had more curves than his Ferrari*

She drives too fast
Christ  he feels her
hell-bent along his veins
all 72000 miles
twice
around the world

*She told him she*
*told him*

Back in his room and his bottle
he looks out the tenth-floor window
at the ocean's rage
hates her at last the way she deserves:
from a cold height on an empty beach
where the breaking waves growl

*like a Ferrari full throttle*

## WINTER IN DETROIT

Stalled in traffic
on Ugly Street  I saw a shivering
underdressed girl  not pretty  swaying across the
way  her heavy boots unlaced
She might have fallen

face forward on our city  which is a hard
one so I thought to pull over to offer her
a lift and show I was still human but what
(I thought again) would people think & maybe she
was an undercover policewoman   when
a large black man appeared and they em
braced   heads quiet on each other's neck

They stayed like that
until I had to move  holding them
in my oval mirror  frozen in the littered
drifts  an unexpected gift
among the wrecks

# A SONG IMPOSSIBLE TO SING

Nothing matters  my darlings  my little ones
though the moon mimes magic in the Spanish moss
and the oaks twist like hearts beside our home

At the end  at bottom  lies the rigid stone
while the brief wind makes the branches toss
in the live oaks twisting by our home

And all falls to zero for our fevered bones
with their burden of a heart like an albatross:
Nothing matters  my darlings  my little ones

I wouldn't have you sorry when I'm gone:
Where nothing's there to gain  where's the loss?
Just the live oaks twisting by our home

and the leaves piling on  and piling on
in our yard where the bright schoolchildren cross
Nothing matters  my darlings  my little ones

It's a pittance that I leave for your inheritance
but the trees have a lesson here for us:
Nothing matters  my darlings  my little ones
to the oaks' twisted hearts around our home

## GANGSTERS

My dream was to sail above the law

sparrow hawk riding spring gusts
giddy with freedom  like Legs Diamond
in the Catskills or the Gallo gang
in Brooklyn when we were young   Sundays
on the way to swim we'd drive past
the abandoned coal yard on Flatbush Avenue
and Father would look serious and say
*That's where Joey Gallo makes moonshine*

and I'd picture a wizard counterfeiting light:
a bloodshot god cranking out the stars . . .
And still  even though we've learned they're all
ignorant scavengers  scuzzy as buzzards

I can itch with envy (bending to peck
my time clock yet again) of Joey and Legs
and Pretty Boy Floyd and all those who shake
their hoods and fly for a feathered minute
among the charged clouds of crime
which shows that while we may grow to know
better  our early humbugs still bubble and squeak
like thugs in the alleys of our bones

unplucked  stinking  and armed to the beak

## MOUNTAIN MAN

As heard in the barbershop


High on Windham Mountain there's a man
who walks so quiet
he can surprise that spookiest of birds
the wild turkey who hears a hunter
spit at fifty yards  sees a eye twitch
at thirty   This trigger-nerved turkey hen
use t'hunters lyin  behind trees  rocks
bushes  always checks and rechecks
everthin:  but the mountain man
sits *in front* of a tree *so still*
that the turkey hen steps on his boots
when she peeks behind it  and the man
grabs her by her scrawny neck
and pops her in his bag slick
as a card trick   He lives
by himself and a pile of bones
in a cave that smells of bear
but that bear ain't comin back nohow
Time was  he had a real home
in Greene County  lived there with
a one-eyed girl who loved t'dance
and sing the old Irish songs
while she worked in their garden
and one day drove off with a en-
cyclopedia salesman in a new Ford who said
she sang like a meadowlark in heaven

The next day the house burnt down
and no one never saw the mountain man
again neither but we know he's up there
because we've seed his tracks in snow
outside the dance hall window
leadin back to the deep woods
and once in a while a skier
feels her skis grow heavy as she glides
through birch and poplar off the beaten trail
and she's scared t'look behind her
knowin the ones who do
never return but lie forever
in the cave and the cold night wind
and the unforgivin hands of the mountain man

## JOHN DOVE

John Dove wanted to make a better world
so he picked this white stone off the lawn
and threw it back on the driveway

A lily  lavender and white  grew
where the stone had been   A neighbor's child
plucked it for her mother who huffed

*There are no lilies around here*   Nevertheless
she stuck it in a vase on the table
and the father that night was duly impressed

Later at the town council he waxed eloquent
(which was most unusual) and exclaimed
*Our school must blossom like a lily on the plain!*

He carried the day  and indeed the school
*did* blossom  opening
to the morning sun   The kids had fun

and one of the students at the new school
grew up to be a Great Woman & the town took pride
in her accomplishments (John Dove having meanwhile died)

## THE FOREST

Everyone's lost in a different forest:

You  for example  trace the clumped moss
clinging to the bark of willows  longing to find
our lost child  the stones sharp and your feet bare
as you pick over needles and narrowing trails
flailing your pale arms through shadows laced with vines
skin and eyes and lungs and heart pierced
till the moss thins at last and you are truly lost

But no moss clings in my forest  Trying
to keep where the trunks are smooth as bars
and the leaves flat in the storm's aftermath
of sun and glisten  I stick to the wide path
waving *goodbyegoodbye* until sunset and first star

and only faintly  when I stop to catch my breath  I hear the crying

It's Happy Hour
and next to me a smoker with yellow
fingers  committing slow
suicide  *Let's Ban Cigarettes!*
(OK: I don't smoke)  Next
to *him*  a woman bends
to her drink  her hands
too shaky for the rimfull glass
*Ban Alcohol!* . . .

(Well, not so fast:
I like my *pivo*)  Next to *her*
a couple seems to be licking the fur
in each other's ear  Everything's
addictive: sex  chocolate  jogging
reading  TV  work  the list
endless  No activity exists
that can't hook a body  ruin
a decent life

It's only human
to be addicted  we're extreme
creatures deep in our twisted genes
dissatisfied with moderate
pleasures  Our natures crave to let
the safe bet go  to misbehave
like needy children: we want
everything *now*  Yugoslavia's
no anomaly . . .

*Ne*  we see a
universal addiction to revenge
that feeds itself and never ends . . .
Meanwhile back at the Bosnian OB
the man next to me's still going
up in smoke   the woman's drowned
in gin  though the couple have flown
to a motel under false names
and the others . . . ?

Well  we're the same
as ever  squinting behind the wheel
behind the times   behind the eight ball
Still   we feel terrific it's two for one
across Amerika:   *This's so much fun
gotta be a crime   Things fall apart  see?
Who knows why?   Luka  makeitadouble
willya?*   No trouble!   Luka slips me
another rhyme

## SUNDAY BRUNCH AT POINT LOOKOUT

You can see five states from here: the Adirondacks
Mount Monadnock and all the farther ranges

The view's spectacular  a smudged palette
of blue gray and green where the Catskills slope
toward deep Schoharie Valley and the Berkshires
hunch like witches in the wings  Our eyes strain
for distance  for white steeples pinning the towns
in place: Oak Hill  Medusa  Grand Gorge

Only if we relax  if our eyes glaze and refocus

can we see the moth trapped between window
and screen  writhing like Laocoön in a web where two flies
have given up the ghost  if flies have ghosts  On the ledge
three feet below a ragged bird  deep blue  lies stunned
or dead  And now we see the ants: *they* know
They march in column  fierce as Genghis Khan . . .

At last the waiter comes  We order  eyes downcast
Eggs Benedict  Bloody Marys  rye toast

## SKYDIVING

Even floating  spread-eagle  from planes
seeing the road swell like a fist
toward your face   becomes commonplace

<pre>
              s           t
samerush     a   e   v   r   i   o
             m       e   g
</pre>

as in the domestication  of adultery
where it seems necessary to grow
increasingly careless forgetting
café matches on the mantel
the smudge on a cuff

the scent
on the neck

un til all the lit tle bones of your life
exPLODE LIKE TOADS
onthecongestedhighway

## OLD BACKBOARDS

They

show different shapes and colors  these
sounding boards for scuffed hearts drib-
bling out the time remaining  score clocks
winding down  Square  oval  rectangular
nailed to garage walls  fat sycamores
barn doors  bolted on poles and posts
even old masts  they weather like the planks
of sunken ships  Cracked  peeling  warped
regaining in dreams the smooth surface
banked on years ago  rust flakes
from their rims  the nets reknit themselves

and wait like lovers to receive

what they were made for  In Windham  Ashland
Sparta  in the four corners of every county
old players sleep like defeated high schools
but the past is a seamless banner spangling
behind us preserving those moments when
pressed between rock and whirlpool
we switched hands and spun it up left-handed
and golden-haired cheerleaders
arched their backs crying our names
with a confidence and joy unmatchable
by the largest paycheck we will ever shoulder

home

## FOR WILLIE MAYS

You gave us a vision of grace  a Greek
statue cast in Africa  touched to life
by a Sistine hand  Week after week
you showed us reflexes keen as a knife
instincts pristine and pure  muscles like stones
Your skill made beauty with a bat and ball
broaching the possibilities in our bones

and we are at least half body  after all

Hence this poem:  beauty deserves permanence  You
who have given so much will someday die
the Say Hey Kid will die  your records too
will fall  tumbled by time  If only I
trying to catch this poem with clumsy hands
could turn  like you  at the crack of the bat
and race headlong fearless toward the white stands

and at the last moment (losing my hat)

reach up and pluck it from the electric air
you would be proud of me  Willie  if you
read poetry  And our poem would be there
integrated in all the schools you never knew
for all the young centerfielders to read and share

## THE CHATTAWAY

We wear our neighborhood tavern
like a pair of old pants:

scratch ourselves  wiggle around
stretch  &  feel good

I think I'll go out now
and put my tavern on

## ON COMPLETING MY PHD
A Professoreal [*sic*] Joke

It's June: the universities
to prove the sun can shine
are hanging their late bloomers
on the academic line

Emerging from the libraries
blinking like a bat
looking at a tree  we wonder
*What the hell is that?*

And I  who've developed
a twitch  a tic  a cough
can't tell if I am finished
or only finished off

I learned Byron had a clubfoot
Nietzsche's health was drastic
Poe was a dipsomaniac
And I'm already spastic

I learned that Shakespeare really lived
so scholars have decided
Though quite a few have studied *me*
they're not as sure that I did

But I can laugh at past mistakes
now that I've reached the harbor
I put my wife on microfilm
and sent her to Ann Arbor

I took my daughter Gretchen out
and my son whatshisname
I lost them in the stacks somehow:
home's never been the same

Now I'm alone  but free at last
to wander in the meadows
the world's leading authority
on Thomas Lovell Beddoes

## OF COURSE
*for Carol*


Could she sing?   Yes  of course  like a robin in April
And is she funny?   Of course!   Wit bubbles out
of her like Dom Pérignon
Red hair?   The reddest  fit for a Queen of Ireland  of course
*Of course?*   Of course 'of course'
all this is so obvious!

And Love  too?
Yes  and *three four five*  keep
counting  love  love of course . . .

## HABIT

Chained to the hands of a clock
like Prometheus to his rock
we forge linkchains
of habitpains
with every ritual morning drive
and every gin we down at 5
each  day  grained  to sifting sand

while  on the other hand

our daughter  who knows tea time is at 4
when she gets thirsty at 3
pushes the hands of the clock an hour ahead
and drinks tea

# TRUCKING

We love the rascally young
because they're poets
(that girl on skates  that boy diving)

Poetry's the rhythmical
re-creation of pizzazz
nothing to do with true
except whereas youth is true

a question of energy & drive:
most young = most alive

Youth & poetry  close to song
just truckin' along  just truckin' along

## WATCHING

. . . watching the World Series
and reading Frank O'Hara
my students' papers flung
across the bed like mortgage threats
I think I'm happy here without you

Today I filled the fireplace with flowers
and poured ashes in all the lumpy vases
that you bought because you love
anything fragile and unpredictable
and I felt pretty happy without you

Tomorrow  I'm going to walk the cat
that you named Dog but always called Charles
and skip stones across the pond
until the pond fills up or all the stones are gone
and I'm completely happy without you . . .

# TRAVELING

The worst thing about traveling is
you don't get to know so many
more people than if you stay
at home   In Paris I
didn't get to know
that boy in the
purple scarf
who played
pinball
games
all
day   In
Rome that
black couple
kissing   London
a stunning brown-eyed
waitress with her front tooth
missing   Munich   Amsterdam
And in seraphic old Siena  where
I stayed burning longer than usual
I didn't get to know at least eight
people I never met  each one of
whom  turning toward me in
repeating rooms
with untouched hands outstretched
I can nev
er for
get

## NODDING

at the edge of this poem
I lose my balance
and fall
in

kingfishers tweak my ringfinger  blueclaws
pry open my toes like clamshells on
mediterranean shoals
they

make no sound it's sunday afternoon calm
surface of water unbroken beside
the shells lie polished
skulls

of drowned buccaneers round as grapefruit
whose seeds split their golden rind
and grow rich
like

ethiopian women their outstretched arms
flush with spindrift
and angel
hair

floating across my eyes
wide open and
deeply
blind

## WALKING BY THE DALÍ MUSEUM

the clouds  on the rainslick

sidewalk  moving faster than I
and once in a while  a bird beneath
my feet  a feeling of speed & light
my heels grow wings I'm dancing on
the sky  above the mailboxhydrantstrees
three smokestacks belching at my toes
so what my toes grow wings my knees grow
wings  my ears my nose my belly and yes

my wings grow wings I feel

like Gulliver bolstered by a flutter
of butterflies above the storm   I feel
free  I feel  free  and now
the butterflies start growing heels
the heels are growing noses/this trip is growing
complicated that's how I know it's

real

## SKIPPING STONES

*for Pete*

Skip
ping stones
seems natur
al  and it is
but the angle from
hand to water must be
acute  the tip of the stone
tilted up just so and the speed
proportional to the stone's weight  the
most pleasing results being widely spaced
hops of five or more and though this isn't high
on the scale of mortal triumphs I have watched on
a Provincetown beach thirteen skips make a grown man cry

# IT BEATS TV

Why do we write poetry?  It beats TV
and keeps us off the streets  out of bars
Lets us wear nose rings and smoke cigars
but mainly it's just vanity:
Look at us  you brutes!  How sensitive  How shy!
How can you stand your jobs  your gray
suits  suburban lawns  scouts and PTA?
O we're so sensitive we think we'll die . . .

All this is true . . . but  in a world
unbeautiful  let's take beauty where
we find it  not search for serpents curled
in common corners  Should we care
that rainbows breed on brackish seas
sunsets are dangerous  and the moon cold?
Honey demands the bodies of dead bees
and poems require poets  to be told

Revile the poets  then  our peacock poses
but though we well deserve to be reviled
out of the dung heap blossom satin roses:
an ugly parent can have a lovely child

## MY POLISH CAP

I found my cap

in a dark alley
in a cold country
I knew it was bugged
but it seemed so unrepressed
folds and lumps unique
as capitalist individualism
its crooked button
weird peak

so we've been together ever since
my hair falling out
left brain warping

Now everyone looks like a spy
Big Business leaves me cold
I'm against the war
don't believe what I'm told
and hold paranoid nuclear fears
because my cap
is a commie conspiracy and
I'm in it

up to my ears

## INDIAN LEGEND

The meeting of the poet Bangshi Das and Kenaram the bandit


The bandit said  *Here I sheathe my sword:*
   sing until I pull it out again
     So Bangshi Das  along with his mild men
       began the bride Behula's song  whose Lord
         was bitten by a snake and died   The den
           of death itself broke for her love and when
             she fell (he sang) Kenaram wept at the word


       He wept until his wound was almost cured:
      Sweet words and music modulate our lives
     by speaking to the blind abandoned child
    curled up within us like a juniper bough
   Behula's song calmed the curving knives
  and Bangshi Das passed safely while the wild
bandit knelt  heart peaceful  at least for now

## THE CAMPAIGN

*for Grover C. Wrenn '64*


Money   that root of all evil   can do
great good when topically applied
Spread it around the Tree of Knowledge
for example   and the Tree's wood will produce
rainbow rings     aliens singing inside

its guardian bark like sublingual tribes

the money   in portfolio or old doubloons
mulching   mulching   opening a golden door
so soon young leaves   (in this metaphor

our own green students)

can dance in the sun like crazed cicadas or
deranged mutants who in the sweet tide of time
will bloom with wisdom   They should of course cry

*Thankyou thankyou Grover!*

as they fly over cove and key   but that
will come later   For now they just say
*Don't crowd me Dude     Give me room*
their rude voices floating like fractal music
over the seeded sands of Boca Ciega Bay

## THE OLD PROFESSOR

Austin Warren's New England Seminar
at the University of Michigan, 1960

Grinding your teeth to brownish stumps
you'd rasp each Tuesday afternoon at three
*Are all the pilgrims safely on the bus?*


Through the open windows  summer dust
mixed with the crump of mowers   Transfixed  we
watched you grind your nubby teeth to stumps


waiting for you to spur us through our jumps
from Cotton Mather up through Emily
*Is every pilgrim happy on this bus?*


We never were sure when you were serious
chaining your Camels unpuritanically
grinding your browning teeth to nubby stumps


and tossing questions far from the syllabus:
*Would you rather live on Broad or Beacon Street?*
*Are Smith and Bradford riding the same bus?*


Wisdom consists in knowing what you love
and how to share it like an autumn feast:
Grinding your nubby teeth to brownish stumps
you spat each pilgrim wiser from the bus

## CHARITY RECITAL (SUITE, 1936: A TRIO)

Liking stories

he studies the program notes:
Milhaud wrote film scores for Jean Renoir
traveled a lot  listened to jazz in Harlem
hated Debussy . . .  Well  so what?
But that's what pulls him:  his story:
*history*  Trapped in this pleated hall
like a weevil in an accordion  no wonder
he feels squeezed  He can barely breathe
among these silver-haired angels
of philanthropy  spreading
on penitential seats like monks in heat

The clarinetist  violinist  both in white:
pale males beside the epigamic splendor
of the pianist's peacock gown  reverse
nature's usual scheme  their shadows
sharp  twitchy as grackles
against the sanded floor  Almost
invisible microphones dip
like spiders toward their heads
To their left a stained flag droops  unmoved
Warhol was nearly right:  no one
in this room will be famous  even briefly

but maybe everyone's a saint
for fifteen minutes  a time when we transcend
our narrow selves  like a trio
coming together once and reaching out
as Francis fed the sparrows
History's the water we walk on
for a while  before sinking to some ocean shelf
to be shuffled  rearranged and played again
like notes in some new suites  rich and strange
(though few will listen  he thinks  smiling
to himself) and  his fifteen minutes up at last

he sleeps

# HYMN 2014

Passing your piano  I turned and sat
to play a hymn or two  and let
the brittle pages flutter at
random  stopping where My Spirit
Longs for Thee glowed in the light
by the fading photo  I'm pretty fit
so don't believe in God yet
nor did you  smiling: 'Not a bit of it!'

My Spirit Longs is written in b-flat
and the hymnal notes read Sadly  instead
of the usual Diminuendo  so my head said
'How can just fingers sing sadness or set
endless loneliness free?'  but then I thought
of you  my only song  and my fingers wept

## LASSING PARK

*In the morning  in all weather*
*laughing at Maxx's familiar bark*
*Jeanne and I walk together*
*to the Old Southeast and Lassing Park*

. . . I will arise and go now  and go to Lassing Park . . .
no   that's a *different* poem 'with clay and wattles made' . . .
But *Lassing Park* is right   In brightening dark
past homes cocooned in mist and shade
we rush to catch the sun lifting from Tampa Bay
our daily doubloon from nature's treasure chest
A colony of ibises measures out the day
pecking their marks  four or five abreast
below live oaks and latticed cabbage palms
those featherdusters for the cobwebbed sky   We turn
north on Beach   the birds ruffling  the bay calm
where dogs  less calm  yank uncombed owners   Headlights burn
through haze   aiming early workers toward highways
and coffee shops  heavy eyes sliding sideways
toward the hungry sun on its own appointed round

*Judge John M. Lassing*
*counted his blessings*
*peered into his heart*
*and gave us his park*

All over the thirsty world its creatures turn toward water
in health and joy   in need   in desperation
Africa already drying   America's shores
polluted by forces quick with false equations

Let's praise our Lassing Parks   save and praise
them all: Vinoy  Straub  Poynter  Pioneer
Demens Landing  Flora Wylie  Elva Rouse
Al Lang  Soreno: just saying the names sheer
pleasure: *Gisella Kopsick Palm Arboretum*!
Elsewhere  oil seeps under sullied beaches  slurring
the seabirds' cries   Smokestacks by Apollo Beach
scrawl toxic messages in the sky  blurring
the sharp rectangles of Tampa's towers
until the air's blown clean by gale or shower
and our park's long view can once again astound

*We* can *save our waterfront parks*
*gods and the government willing*
*Heed the wild green parrots' squawk:*
No drilling!  No drilling!  No drilling!

O Lassing mine O Lassing yours O Lassing ours forever!
Its cedars  hawthorn  sweet bays  pine  preserve our civic health
by opening their fragrant arms to birds of every feather:
white  brown  black  and  mixed: our integrated wealth
strolls along the margin of the bay   We breathe
the park's green acres  soothing water   Our hearts
rise with the tide  with the golden trumpet tree
honey-throated as a tipsy robin  Wounds start
to heal as joggers  soldiers  workers young and old
pass on every side: *Hey Hey! Good mornin'! Where you been?*
The world's wide and good  or could be: good as the gold
that's dusted on our parks by sun and wind

Through hurricanes of man and gods  through kind and wicked weather—
O Lassing mine O Lassing yours O Lassing ours forever—
May St. Petersburg's waterfront parks for all time shield our town . . .

*In the evening  herons nest*
*in oak trees bending toward the west*
*and the moon and stars on their hallowed arc*
*keep their nightly watch over Lassing Park*

# EPITAPH

*Below these live oak branches lie*
*a poet's ashes  pale and dry*
*He loved the feel of books in hand*
*but saw his words*
*as driven sand*

*Still  he dreams  as you pass by*
*although you may be far from home*
*that if you pause to read this poem*
*the leaves might nod*
*and understand*

# Acknowledgments

Grateful acknowledgment is made to the following publications in which some of these poems have appeared:

*Amber Mist*: "Walking by the Dalí Museum," under the title "Walking on Birds"; *Antioch Review*: "Cassandra in the Library," under the title "Blood Is Simple," and "On Completing My PhD"; *Cantilever*: "Traveling"; *CCL Newsletter*: "Father and Child"; *Christian Century*: "John Dove"; *Crosscurrents*: "Old Backboards"; *Eckerd Review*: "The Campaign," "Emily Dickinson Thinks about Buying a Ribbon," and "Nodding"; *Ekphrasis*: "Impressionist"; *El Urogallo*: "Nodding," in Spanish titled "Al Borde"; *Enigmatist*: "Of Course"; *Fiddler Crab*: "Trucking"; *5 A.M.*: "Skipping Stones"; *Gulf Stream*: "For Willie Mays"; *Heliotrope*: "Sky-Diving"; *Laurel Review*: "It Beats TV" and "The Lover"; *Lightning Key Review*: "Heartworld"; *The Line-Up: Poems on Crime*: "The Firebug"; *mOOn*: "D. E. A. T. H."; *OCHO*: "The Family Megashelter" and "Front-Rhymed Easter Anti-Sonnet"; *Offshoots (Geneva)*: "Sunday Brunch at Point Lookout"; *Plume*: "The Floss-Silk Tree and the Philodendron" and "Sic Transit Gloria Mundi"; *Poetry Now*: "Indian Legend"; *Red Mud Review*: "Charity Recital"; *Sandhill Review*: "Gangsters," "Lucky Bones," and "The Devil's Paintbrush"; *Saw Palm*: "Mirror Lake" and "Old Houses"; *Smartishpace*: "The Activist"; *Snake Nation Review*: "Ants, Ants"; *South Florida Review*: "Habit"; *Stringtown*: "Mountain Man"; *Tampa Review*: "Drive-by Shooting," "Epitaph," and "Habemus Papam"; *White Pelican Review*: "Unbearable Lightness"; *Windless Orchard*: "The Chattaway."

Seventeen of these poems appeared in a chapbook, *Lassing Park*, published by Yellow Jacket Press (Tampa, Florida) in 2011.